Religious Freedom Today
The Catholic View

by
John Newton

with a Preface by David Alton
(Lord Alton of Liverpool)

*All booklets are published thanks to the
generous support of the members of the
Catholic Truth Society*

CATHOLIC TRUTH SOCIETY
PUBLISHERS TO THE HOLY SEE

Contents

ISBN 978 1 78469 069 4

Preface

In western democracies the debate about religious freedom revolves around secular and religious values, but for millions of others religious freedom is defined by suppression and persecution. The twentieth century saw more Christian martyrs than the previous nineteen centuries combined. More than half of the world's six billion inhabitants live in countries where being a Christian could cost you your life.

When the Council Fathers met at the Second Vatican Council to address the topic of religious freedom, they did so in the proximity of the tomb of St Peter - who, as well as being the first Pope, gave his life for the Faith. To this day, in our Catholic liturgies we commemorate the sacrifices of the Church's early martyrs: Peter and Paul, Clement, Cecilia, Felicity, Agatha and the many others. Their refusal to capitulate to the civil authorities in religious matters brought them a martyr's crown.

The document the Fathers produced, *Dignitatis Humanae*, stresses the duty of the believer to search for truth and the simultaneous duty to disavow any form of coercion. It asserts the centrality of the proclamation of human dignity - a dignity which had all too often been violated in the first half of that bloody century. The Council Fathers had learnt a great deal from the experiences of

Nazism and Communism. Emerging from the experiences of a suffering Church, *Dignitatis Humanae* became the Second Vatican Council's response to the erupting challenges of the time.

Indeed, *Dignitatis Humanae* speaks forcefully to our own times. It is addressed to the whole world - to believer and non-believer alike. It speaks eloquently to contemporary totalitarian regimes in countries like China and North Korea and to radical Islamist states such as Sudan. It reminds the secularist that God wants no compulsory conversion and governments that they do not have the right to suppress the freedom of religious profession and practice.

Yet despite the prophetic message of *Dignitatis Humanae*, religious liberty is an often neglected part of the Church's teaching. But it needs to be heard. I am therefore delighted that Dr Newton has produced this summary of *Dignitatis Humanae* and other Church teaching on the subject. As a key member of Aid to the Church in Need's Press and Information team, he is keenly aware that every single day Christians, and others, experience harassment and persecution in countries where freedom of religion is not respected - and I am proud to be a trustee of Aid to the Church in Need (UK) and support its vital work helping our suffering brothers and sisters around the world.

It is my hope that this booklet will make Catholics - and indeed all those of good will - aware of why religious freedom is of vital importance to today's world, and will inspire readers to reach out in compassion to those denied this basic human right.

David Alton

Introduction[1]

"In the world today freedom of religion is often talked about rather than put into practice. Indeed, it is forcibly subjected to threats of various kinds and not seldom violated." Unfortunately, one does not have to look very far to find examples which illustrate these words of Pope Francis.

For example, in Pakistan a Christian man, Sawan Masih, was sentenced to death for blasphemy in March 2014. Twelve months previously, 178 homes and two churches were torched when a three-thousand-strong mob attacked a Christian area, called Joseph Colony, following accusations that Mr Masih had uttered blasphemy against the Muslim prophet Muhammed. One Joseph Colony resident said: "We were working [just] like every day, when we started to hear a noise, and suddenly a wall of people fell upon the colony. They threw acid and stoned our houses, then set them on fire. The authorities intervened only when everything was destroyed".[2] Mr Masih maintained his innocence during his year-long trial, claiming that the allegation was prompted by a property dispute.[3] Speaking from death row in November 2014, he said: "God knows me, he knows that I am innocent".[4] Nor is this an isolated case. Christians and other religious minorities in the country - including Shi'a Muslims - have suffered similar attacks and court sentences over the years following accusations of blasphemy.

Nor is religious intolerance restricted to countries like Pakistan. In North Korea there is practically no freedom of belief or practice for any religious group. Officially an atheist state, citizens attempting to worship God can face severe fines and penalties. Even foreign aid workers can run foul of the authorities if they are linked to religious groups: in January 2015, Canadian Presbyterian minister Hyeon Soo Lim, who had been carrying out humanitarian work with orphans and the elderly, was seized by authorities without any reason being given.[5] And in numerous cases religious activity has been punished by imprisonment in the country's internment camps, where prisoners face starvation, forced labour, routine beatings, systematic torture, and arbitrary executions.[6] In November 2013, the first large scale executions under new leader Kim Jong-un took place in a number of cities and eighty people were killed, among them Christians who were sentenced to death for possessing Bibles.[7]

Encroachments on religious freedom can also occur on a much smaller scale. Coptic Orthodox Christian Nadia Eweida was asked by her employer British Airways (BA) to remove the crucifix she wore when working at Heathrow Airport. She refused - since Muslim, Sikh and Buddhist colleagues were permitted to wear religious clothing and symbols - and was put on unpaid leave. Ms Eweida fought the case all the way to the European Court of Human Rights, which in 2013 finally ruled that BA had not struck a fair balance between Ms Eweida's religious beliefs and the company's wish to "project a certain corporate image".[8] It may seem a relatively minor incident, indeed it is trivial compared to those occurring in Pakistan or North Korea, but it illustrates the kinds of issues faced by religious believers in western democracies.

Time after time modern societies around the world refuse to let individuals exercise their religious beliefs in a number of different ways. When Pope Francis spoke on the subject he may have had in mind major violations of the kind we find in Pakistan and North Korea. The Holy Father continued:

> The serious affronts inflicted on this primary right are a source of grave concern and must see the unanimous reaction of the world's countries in reaffirming the intangible dignity of the human person, against every attack. One and all are duty bound to defend religious freedom and to promote it for everyone. The shared protection of this moral good is also a guarantee of the entire community's growth and development.[9]

As we will see the Church teaches that all religious believers, regardless of creed, should be free from state coercion in religious matters, and not be forced to act against their consciences.

Human Dignity

The dignity of the human individual is the starting point of Catholic thought on religious freedom. This is reflected in the very title of the Second Vatican Council's document on the subject *Dignitatis Humanae* - which translates into English as "human dignity". The problem of religious communities and individual believers not being allowed to freely practise their faith came to the fore in the twentieth century, and the Church's Second Vatican Council which met in the 1960s addressed this new situation. The Decree on the Right of the Person and of Communities to Social and Civil Freedom, or *Dignitatis Humanae,* is the touchstone for all contemporary Catholic thinking on religious freedom in modern societies. So in looking at the Church's teaching on the issue we will return to this key document time and time again, and much of the material in the following pages will be taken from it, while drawing on a broad range of other material from papal encyclicals and other Church sources.

The image of God

In the Catholic view, the dignity of the human person comes from us having been created in the image and likeness of God.[10] In the book of Genesis the story is told of how God made humanity and describes how, having made man and woman as the pinnacle of creation, God gifted us and blessed us:

> Then God said, "Let us make Man in our image, after our likeness; and let them have dominion over the fish of the sea, and over the birds of the air, and over the cattle, and over all the earth, and over every creeping thing that creeps upon the earth." So God created Man in his own image, in the image of God he created him; male and female he created them.[11]

Having created Man in his own image and likeness, God endowed him with intelligence and freedom, and made him lord over creation. Pope St John XXIII saw this proclaimed in the Psalms where it says: "Thou hast made him a little less than the angels: thou hast crowned him with glory and honor, and hast set him over the works of thy hands. Thou hast subjected all things under his feet." [12] We are not mere creatures, rather we have been made to be like God.

A spiritual likeness

The image of God within humankind is not a physical image, but rather refers to our souls' ability to reason and choose.[13] Of course we have the ability to choose wrongly, as illustrated by the episode later in Genesis where Adam and Eve chose to eat the forbidden fruit, but this does not

It follows that a wrong is done when government imposes upon its people, by force or fear or other means, the profession or repudiation of any religion, or when it hinders men from joining or leaving a religious community. All the more is it a violation of the will of God and of the sacred rights of the person and the family of nations when force is brought to bear in any way in order to destroy or repress religion, either in the whole of mankind or in a particular country or in a definite community.[44]

While the Church recognises the need for the state to use law to regulate human activity, which may involve proscribing religious activities, in all cases this must be reasonable (see the section "Rights and Responsibilities" below). In Communist and Marxist regimes the regulation of religious groups has more to do with imposing the state ideology than protecting the common good. The problems of totalitarianism were enumerated by Pope St John Paul II, who had lived under the oppression of a Soviet regime in Poland. As the pontiff pointed out, such regimes justify their practice by asserting that their actions are done for the good of the state, so certain freedoms are curtailed in order to promote the political elite's ideology.[45] Such repression in the name of the greater good continues today.

Coercion is not restricted to states based on Marxist principles, nor indeed is it always driven by governments.

In many cases it is groups or individuals acting on their own initiative whom the state either does not have the ability to stop or for a complex series of motives refrains from restraining. The former appears to have been the case in Iraq. While the world's media focused on the attacks by Islamist extremists which started in summer 2014, attacks that drove more than 250,000 people from their homes in the Nineveh Plains in the north of the country, Iraq's minority religious communities have long been targeted by extremist groups. To highlight just one such incident: more than fifty-two people were killed and upwards of seventy injured in the 31st October 2010 siege of Baghdad's Our Lady of Salvation Syriac-Catholic Cathedral. Jihadists attacked the Sunday evening service, holding Mass-goers hostage for four hours, before blowing themselves up using the suicide bombs in their jackets. As Pope Benedict XVI noted in his words of consolation for the Christian community: "In the days that followed, other attacks ensued, even on private homes, spreading fear within the Christian community and a desire on the part of many to emigrate in search of a better life."[46] Extremists targeted families who had lost loved ones in the attack on the cathedral - identifying their homes by mourning signs at their houses. In these attacks three people died and twenty-six were injured.[47] The Chaldean procurator to the Holy See, Monsignor Philip Najim, described how these were not new phenomena and that for many years Christians had lived with"[a]rmed groups [that] go into neighbourhoods where Christians live and kill indiscriminately everyone they find in their way…These are coldblooded murders in broad daylight, before dozens of witnesses, as if these groups wanted to show that they can act with impunity; that they are in control of the city."[48]

There are many other instances of coercion one could mention. For example, in India militant nationalists attacked Christians in Odisha in August 2008. During the pogroms at least ninety people were killed, more than fifty thousand driven from their homes, and around one hundred and seventy Christian places of worship were destroyed.[49] In Sri Lanka and Burma (Myanmar), Buddhism has become intertwined with militant nationalism leading to both Christian and Muslim communities being targeted.[50] Members of the Burmese army have forced or pressurised people living in the country's tribal provinces to abandon their beliefs and embrace Buddhism. And it is estimated that between mid-2012 and mid-2013 more than five thousand Rohingya Muslims were killed by the Burmese military.[51] Even western countries are not immune from coercing religious groups to make them act in accordance with state-sponsored orthodoxy, although it must again be stressed that the problems faced in western countries are on an altogether different scale. However, while these problems may not be as extreme, this does not make them any less real. In the United States of America, Catholic foster care and adoption services in Boston, San Francisco, the State of Illinois, and the District of Columbia (where the capital Washington is located) were forced to stop operating when their licences were revoked or their government contracts were terminated (or in some cases both), because they would only place children with married couples, refusing to place them with either unmarried cohabitating couples or same-sex couples.[52]

Rights and Responsibilities

As indicated above, the rights of believers and religious groups within a society are not unfettered and do confer certain duties and responsibilities upon them. It is not outside the scope of the state to impose "regulatory norms" which are genuinely for the "common good" - and don't merely reflect the majority will that may be antagonistic to the rights or aspirations of minority groups.[53] "A religious belief should not be perceived or considered as harmful or offensive simply because it is different from that of the majority."[54] In seeking the protection of the common good, the state has the right to "defend itself against possible abuses committed on the pretext of freedom of religion".[55] As Pope Benedict XVI taught:

> The exploitation of religious freedom to disguise hidden interests, such as the subversion of the established order, the hoarding of resources or the grip on power of a single group, can cause enormous harm to societies. Fanaticism, fundamentalism and practices contrary to human dignity can never be justified, even less so in the name of religion.[56]

Nor should the advancement of religious liberty be seen as an excuse for libertinism or law breaking in any form. *Dignitatis Humanae* teaches very clearly that "the moral principle of personal and social responsibility is to be observed…[individuals are] bound by the moral law to have respect both for the rights of others and for their own duties toward others and for the common welfare of all. Men are to deal with their fellows in justice and civility".[57] The right to religious liberty then does not provide believers with a moral licence to act however they want to, rather it provides immunity from external constraint and coercion in religious matters by political authorities.[58] The ideal is that individuals should act on their own judgement, "making use of a responsible freedom" and motivated by a sense of duty.[59] Indeed, the aim of religious freedom ought to be that individuals "come to act with greater responsibility in fulfilling their duties in community life."[60]

Dignitatis Humanae foresees a reciprocal relationship between the Church and the state whereby the state grants liberty for religions to follow their own paths, except where the good of society genuinely requires it *by an objective standard*. The state is not to discriminate against religious believers but rather uphold equality of both believers and non-believers before the law.[61] Indeed, a state "would clearly transgress the limits set to its power, were it to presume to command or inhibit acts that are religious."[62]

Freedom for Families

Dignitatis Humanae also states that the family "has the right freely to live its own domestic religious life under the guidance of parents."[63] Why are the rights of the family singled out? Because the Church sees the family is "a society in its own original right" - indeed it is the key building block of any religious society. The important role parents play in transmitting the Faith and values to the coming generations is a scriptural idea that goes right back to Abraham in the book of Genesis. When describing why he has called him, God says: "I have chosen him, that he may charge his children and his household after him to keep the way of the Lord by doing righteousness and justice; so that the Lord may bring to Abraham what he has promised him."[64] Abraham and Sarah were chosen to pass on the values of morality, justice, and righteousness to their descendants, and all parents are called to pass on these core values to their children.[65]

Rights of parents

Parents also have the right to determine their children's religious education in accordance with their own beliefs. This should be far from controversial as the Universal Declaration of Human Rights makes it plain that "Parents have a prior right to choose the kind of education that shall be given to their children."[66] *Dignitatis Humanae* develops this theme in the religious sphere, stating that parents have the right to determine their children's religious education in accordance with their own beliefs, and it is worth considering the Church's teaching regarding this aspect of family life:

> *The family has a completely original and irreplaceable role in raising children.* The parents' love, placing itself at the service of children to draw forth from them ("*educere*")[67] the best that is in them, finds its fullest expression precisely in the task of educating. "As well as being a *source*, the parents' love is also the *animating* principle and therefore the *norm* inspiring and guiding all concrete educational activity, enriching it with the values of kindness, constancy, goodness, service, disinterestedness and self-sacrifice that are the most precious fruit of love"... Parents have the duty and right to impart a religious education and moral formation to their children, a right the State cannot annul but which it must respect and promote. This is a primary right that the family may not neglect or delegate.[68]

Within a civil multi-faith society this would mean, amongst other things, the right of all parents to educate their children in accordance with their own deeply held convictions - be they religious or otherwise.

---

[67] The English word education comes from the Latin *educere*, which means "to draw forth".

Public support

Dignitatis Humanae says that governments should therefore acknowledge parents' right to choose their children's education. Nor should states impose disadvantages on parents who exercise these choices by sending their children to faith-based schools, as this would be an implicit form of coercion, by making it more difficult to educate their children in their religion. Moreover public authorities must see to it that "public subsidies are so allocated that parents are truly free to exercise this right without incurring unjust burdens. Parents should not have to sustain, directly or indirectly, extra charges which would deny or unjustly limit the exercise of this freedom".[69] Equally, children should not be forced to attend lessons, or other forms of instruction, which contradict their religious values. *Dignitatis Humanae* also condemns the imposition of a single system of education, from which all religious formation is excluded.[70] The Church cannot tolerate the situation which existed under Communism in Eastern Europe whereby atheism was indoctrinated as part of a child's schooling - the beliefs of the state overriding and utterly disregarding the wishes of the parents; nor is it right for any group to deny Catholic schools the right to teach about the Faith.[71] In Venezuela, under the late President Hugo Chavez's programme of Bolivarian socialism, there were several attempts by the state to restrict the activities of the Catholic Church, including a 2009 education bill which attempted to remove religious education from all the country's schools - including Church schools.[72] Nor are threats to religious choice in schools necessarily the preserve of Marxist regimes. In 2014 Joël Mergui, president of the Central Consistory of the Jews of France, expressed fears that proposals to extend secularism in France's state schools would restrict existing rights, such as parents being able to take children out of class to participate in major religious festivals.[73]

Why does the Church place such a stress on the importance of education as part of parents' rights to raise their children in the Faith? To some degree it has to do with passing on the Faith's beliefs and values, but it is about more than just that. Pope Benedict XVI explained that education was central to establishing the values within society that lead to equality in societies and the common good. He called religious education "the highway which leads new generations to see others as their brothers and sisters, with whom they are called to journey and work together…". Furthermore, reiterating the teaching of the Scriptures that the social, cultural, moral and spiritual formation and growth of children begins within the family, he stressed that:

> Parents must be always free to transmit to their children, responsibly and without constraints, their heritage of

faith, values and culture…Wisdom suggests that this is the road to building a strong and fraternal social fabric, in which young people can be prepared to assume their proper responsibilities in life, in a free society, and in a spirit of understanding and peace…[74]

Freedom to proclaim the Good News

Up until this point we have been considering the general idea of religious freedom, which is expressed and argued "from the point of view of natural law, that is to say from the 'purely human' position, on the basis of the premises given by Man's own experience, his reason and his sense of human dignity"[75] - although this is, of course, informed by the Church's worldview as drawn from Scripture and Tradition. Nevertheless, the aim is to establish an argument based on natural law: that is, on universal principles that can be deduced from a rational observation of the world around us, and will be understood by those who think through the arguments. But *Dignitatis Humanae* also looks at the unique position of the Church as divinely founded by Jesus Christ, the incarnate Son of God, and as a consequence she uniquely claims for herself the right to follow Our Lord's teaching.

> In human society and in the face of government, the Church claims freedom for herself in her character as a spiritual authority, established by Christ the Lord, upon which there rests, by divine mandate, the duty of going out into the whole world and preaching the Gospel to every creature.[76]

More than religious freedom, which is a right based on natural law, Jesus Christ demands for his Church *libertas ecclesiae* - the liberty of the Church - which is a supernatural right, founded upon divine revelation, to carry out the mission he committed to her.[77] The Church has been entrusted with the Deposit of Faith which she must faithfully transmit, like a good mother, to her children, and also make clear to all who enquire after it.

The Church then has a mandate to profess the truth it received from the Apostles. In connection with this, a couple of points should be noted:

Firstly, that just as it abhors all religious groups using coercion or "dishonourable persuasion" to acquire members, so it would abhor such means being used to make converts to Christianity. Indeed it stresses that an individual must freely respond to the call of God. *Dignitatis Humanae* also makes it very clear that just as no one should be coerced by civil authorities in matters of religion, so no one should be coerced to accept the Catholic Faith either. As Pope Leo XIII wrote: "It is one of the major tenets of Catholic doctrine that Man's response to God in faith must be free: therefore no one is to be forced to embrace the Christian faith against his own will."[78] Opposition to this way of forcing belief is, again, drawn from the ancient teaching of the Church. "[I]n fact, the Church is wont to take earnest heed that no one shall be forced to embrace the Catholic faith against his will, for, as St Augustine wisely reminds us, 'Man cannot believe otherwise than of his own will'."[79] The pontiff went on to say that, as part of its commitment to avoiding all forms of coercion and respecting people's freedom of conscience, the Church teaches that,

> in spreading religious faith and in introducing religious practices, everyone ought at all times to refrain from any manner of action which might seem to carry a hint of coercion or of a kind of persuasion that would be dishonourable or unworthy, especially when dealing with poor or uneducated people. Such a manner of action would have to be considered an abuse of one's right and a violation of the right of others.[80]

Evangelisation and Religious Freedom

Secondly, there are those who question whether evangelisation isn't, in and of itself, a violation of religious freedom, or at least a sign of disrespect for others' beliefs. On this point, it is worth reflecting on Pope Paul VI's words about the contradiction which some people perceived between religious liberty and the proclamation of the Gospel:

> [O]ne too frequently hears it said, in various terms, that to impose a truth, be it that of the Gospel, or to impose a way, be it that of salvation, cannot but be a violation of

religious liberty. Besides, it is added, why proclaim the Gospel when the whole world is saved by uprightness of heart? We know likewise that the world and history are filled with "seeds of the Word"; is it not therefore an illusion to claim to bring the Gospel where it already exists in the seeds that the Lord himself has sown?

Anyone who takes the trouble to study in the Council's documents the questions upon which these excuses draw too superficially will find quite a different view. It would certainly be an error to impose something on the consciences of our brethren. But to propose to their consciences the truth of the Gospel and salvation in Jesus Christ, with complete clarity and with a total respect for the free options which it presents - "without coercion, or dishonourable or unworthy pressure" - far from being an attack on religious liberty is fully to respect that liberty, which is offered the choice of a way that even non-believers consider noble and uplifting.[81]

The Catholic Church continues to believe and teach that it was founded by Jesus on the rock of the Apostle Peter and has the duty imposed upon it by the Son of God himself to proclaim the Good News. While this must be done in a way that is worthy of the Gospel and does not compromise its values, the Church must cleave to the deposit of Faith handed down to us from the Apostles, and be a channel of God's grace to the world.[82]

Did Vatican II break with Tradition?

While it should be plain from Pope Paul VI's words above that Vatican II reaffirmed the Catholic Church's traditional teaching about proclaiming the Faith, nevertheless it is frequently alleged that *Dignitatis Humanae* broke with previous teaching about religious liberty. This is advanced by two different groups - approvingly by those who see the Church as having adopted a pluralistic and relativistic outlook and disapprovingly by those who see the Church as having turned its back on previous pronouncements on the subject. Neither assessment is true. As Fr John Courtney Murray, the American Jesuit who oversaw the third and fourth drafts of the document that eventually became *Dignitatis Humanae*, wrote:

> I think that these objections were based upon a failure to examine the document very closely. Put it this way: the document always granted that the Roman Catholic Church and all other Churches have an equal footing *in human society*. Thus neither the Roman Catholic Church nor the individual Catholic nor the other Churches nor their members are to be subjected to coercion in religious matters…[but] the Church claims immunity from coercion on grounds of its divine

mandate received from Christ himself: "Go into the whole world and preach the Gospel to all creatures" (*Mk* 16: 16). On the other hand, the Church asserts the right of other individuals and of other religious Communities to religious freedom on the grounds of the dignity of the human person…Hence, the charge of religious indifferentism is completely invalid.[83]

When *Dignitatis Humanae* was being written, the world had changed and the Church was addressing a new situation, taking seriously the assessment of Pope St John XXIII that "we are confronted in this modern age with a form of society which is evolving on entirely new social and political lines" and addressing that situation.[84] The twentieth century saw significant changes in the models of government in countries across the world, and the decline of Catholic states. In many western countries universal participation in the electoral process was established for the first time; in other places both far right and far left ideologies led to the establishment of dictatorships or *de facto* one-party states. Even in many countries in the West, the introduction of democracy was accompanied by secularisation and growing hostility towards any special recognition for the Church, even in countries with a sizeable Catholic population which had been traditionally sympathetic to the Faith. These shifts in the political landscape led to changes in the relationship between religious groups and the states, and in some places saw the repression of some aspect or aspects of the Church and its members.

Responding to these shifts, the Second Vatican Council deliberated on "the right of the person and of communities to social and civil freedom in religious matters" and, as we have noted, on 7th December 1965 issued its declaration on that very issue: *Dignitatis Humanae*. It specifically addressed the situation of individual believers and religious communities in the societies of the modern world, and it specifically refers to social and civil matters. Therefore to interpret correctly the text of *Dignitatis Humanae*, "it is essential to have this in mind: that *Dignitatis Humanae* refers to a civil right of freedom from coercion and excludes the idea that this right is based on a non-existent equal value or truth of all religions".[85]

No change in teaching

It is important to note that from its opening paragraph *Dignitatis Humanae* stresses that it does not intend to change Church teaching. So, after stating what I would argue is the document's key theme - that "Religious freedom…has to do with immunity from coercion in civil society" - it immediately adds "Therefore it leaves untouched traditional Catholic doctrine on the moral duty of men and societies toward the true religion and toward the one Church of Christ." Properly understood and rightly interpreted, *Dignitatis Humanae* is in full continuity with the previous magisterium of the Church and must be read that way. The aim was not to promote indifferentism in matters of religion - described by Pope Gregory XVI in *Mirari Vos* as the belief "that by any profession of faith whatsoever, the eternal salvation of the soul can be attained" - rather it was to establish tolerance and oppose state coercion in religious matters. As Pope Benedict XVI stressed, while religious freedom is one of the fundamental human rights, nevertheless "religious freedom does not mean religious indifferentism, nor does it imply that all religions are equal".[86]

Indeed, as we have said, *Dignitatis Humanae* stresses that nothing contained within it contradicts previous teachings. Rather it states that "the council professes its belief that God himself has made known to mankind the way in which men are to serve him, and thus be saved in Christ and come to blessedness. We believe that this one true religion subsists in the Catholic and Apostolic Church, to which the Lord Jesus committed the duty of spreading it abroad among all men."[87] The Catholic Church then believes that it is not one religion among many, but the one true religion.

Is Religious Freedom an International Human Right?

As *Dignitatis Humanae* noted in the 1960s, "religious freedom has already been declared to be a civil right in most constitutions, and it is solemnly recognised in international documents."[88] It was, of course, referring to Article 18 of the Universal Declaration of Human Rights, which was passed by the United Nations General Assembly on 10th December 1948. The Declaration of Human Rights, which was part and parcel of the setting up of the United Nations Organisation, aimed to draw a line under the dehumanising experiences of the Second World War and the horrors seen under extreme political systems by providing a standard for states to measure themselves against. Article 18 reads:

Everyone has the right to freedom of thought, conscience and religion; this right includes freedom to change his religion or belief, and freedom, either alone or in community with others and in public or private, to manifest his religion or belief in teaching, practice, worship and observance.

The UN's Declaration was generally, but cautiously, welcomed by the Catholic Church. Pope St John XXIII wrote:

We are, of course, aware that some of the points in the declaration did not meet with unqualified approval in some quarters; and there was justification for this. Nevertheless, we think the document should be considered a step in the right direction, an approach toward the establishment of a juridical and political ordering of the world community. It is a solemn recognition of the personal dignity of every human being; an assertion of everyone's right to be free to seek out the truth, to follow moral principles, discharge the duties imposed by justice, and lead a fully human life. It also recognised other rights connected with these.[89]

As Pope Benedict said in a 2008 address to the UN, echoing good Pope John's words: "Through the United Nations, states have established universal objectives which, even if they do not coincide with the total common good of the human family, undoubtedly represent a fundamental part of that good."[90] Pope Benedict went on to outline, not only the basis of the Declaration in natural law, but also to expound the dangers of departing from this basis:

It is evident, though, that the rights recognised and expounded in the Declaration apply to everyone by virtue of the common origin of the person, who remains the high-point of God's creative design for the world and for history. They are based on the natural law inscribed on human hearts and present in different cultures and civilisations. Removing human rights from this context would mean restricting their range and yielding to a relativistic conception, according to which the meaning and interpretation of rights could vary and their universality would be denied in the name of different cultural, political, social and even religious outlooks. This great variety of viewpoints must not be allowed to obscure the fact that not only rights are universal, but so too is the human person, the subject of those rights.[91]

Such basic rights are denied on a number of different grounds, and the right to manifest one's religion is a frequent casualty. According to one analysis, about seventy percent of the world's population are living in countries "where governments imposed high restrictions on religion or where there were high levels of religious hostilities in society". This is despite the fact that in seventy-two percent of the world's countries the constitution (or legal equivalent) provides for "freedom of religion" or included language used in the UN's Universal Declaration of Human Rights. But then it found that in fifty-six percent of countries the constitution or basic law included stipulations that appear to qualify or substantially contradict the concept of "freedom of religion".[92] Indeed as Archbishop Silvano M. Tomasi - the permanent observer of the Holy See to the United Nations - has noted: "In many countries, however, the gap is growing between widely accepted stated principles, and their daily application on the ground."[93]

Pope St John Paul II reflected that while much good had come from the Declaration, nevertheless, in many ways people were paying lip service to it without implementing the reality that it called for:

> While sharing the joy of all people of good will, of all people who truly love justice and peace, at [the recognition of human rights on an international level], the Church, aware that the "letter" on its own can kill, while only "the spirit gives life", must continually ask, together with these people of good will, whether the Declaration of Human Rights and the acceptance of their "letter" mean everywhere also the actualisation of their "spirit". Indeed, well-founded fears arise that very often we are still far from this actualisation and that at times the spirit of social and public life is painfully opposed to the declared "letter" of human rights.[94]

The horrors of Communism

One example of states denying human rights was only too well known to the Polish Pope who had lived under the restrictions of Communism. Even though in Poland the Church was not as totally cowed as in other Soviet countries, it was rigidly restricted. Reflecting on the problems experienced under Communism and Fascism in its various forms, Pope St John Paul II wrote:

Already in the first half of [the twentieth] century, when various State totalitarianisms were developing, which, as is well known, led to the horrible catastrophe of war, the Church clearly outlined her position with regard to these regimes that to all appearances were acting for a higher good, namely the good of the State, while history was to show instead that the good in question was only that of a certain party, which had been identified with the State. In reality, those regimes had restricted the rights of the citizens, denying them recognition precisely of those inviolable human rights that have reached formulation on the international level in the middle of our century.[95]

The Universal Declaration of Human Rights was, in part, a response to the horrors of the early twentieth century, which Pope St John Paul II had experienced first-hand. In Eastern Europe the spread of Communism led to numerous priests being arrested, killed or sent to the gulags. To give one example, Archbishop Kazimierz Świątek, who died in July 2011 at the age of ninety-six, was the only priest of his diocese to survive the Communist persecution. In April 1941, as a young assistant parish priest, he was arrested by the NKVD, the Soviet secret police, and sentenced to death. He was imprisoned in a death cell in a prison camp in Brest, a city in modern-day Belarus, close to the border with Poland, for two months, but managed to escape execution. He was set free as, before the sentence could be carried out, the German army pushed forward into the Soviet Union.

Until the end of the German occupation the then Fr Świątek worked as parish priest in Pruzana, near Brest, staying there after it was occupied by the Red Army. But in December 1944 he was arrested again and in July 1945 was sentenced to ten years' forced labour in Maryinsk gulag. Fr Świątek said:

> It was a death sentence. We worked in temperatures down to minus forty degrees, felling timber, and slept as many as three hundred people at a time, in a Semlanka - a hole in the ground with a makeshift covering - without any light and without anything. They told us a bullet would be wasted on us, since we would die here anyway, and so until then we could carry on working. Exhaustion, hunger and cold brought death to many. In the mornings, before we began work, the dead were thrown out into the snow. The wolves came in the night and ate up the bodies. When they saw I was still alive after three years, they sent me to Vorkuta. There it was winter for twelve months of the year.

After the death of Communist leader Stalin in 1953, Fr Świątek was released and went to work as parish priest in Pinsk (in modern-day Belarus). In 1991, after Belarus became independent from the Soviet Union, Fr Świątek was appointed Archbishop of Minsk-Mohilev and Apostolic Administrator of Pinsk by Pope St John Paul II, and made a Cardinal in 1994. Asked by Aid to the Church in Need's Neville Kyrke-Smith how his faith had survived after everything he had been through, the Cardinal replied: "If you believe in God, and God is in you, you can do everything. It is very simple."[96]

Ecumenism of Suffering

According to one estimate, more than twenty million Christians were killed in the USSR, but it is impossible to ever know exactly how many people were killed for their faith in Our Lord Jesus Christ, or indeed for holding other beliefs forbidden by Communist authorities. Catholics, Orthodox and members of other Christian communities found themselves together in the gulags. Cardinal Lubomyr Husar, the retired head of the Ukrainian Greek-Catholic Church - an Eastern-rite Church in full communion with the Pope - speaks of the "ecumenism of the Gulag", as under the Soviets, Christians of all denominations were united in suffering.[97]

One could point to similar situations in the world today where Christians are brought closer together through the persecution or oppression that they experience. In Egypt, Catholics and Orthodox suffered side by side when rising Islamist extremism targeted believers of all Churches equally. The situation for Christians in Egypt has never been good: there have always been reports of young Coptic women being abducted[98] and sporadic attacks on churches, but in the aftermath of President Mohamed Morsi's fall from power in 2013, problems reached a new peak. Estimates indicate that more than hundred churches, monasteries and other Church institutions were torched, destroyed, or attacked.[99] As Pope Francis said to the head of the Coptic Orthodox Church, Pope Tawadros II, when they met for the first time in May 2013:

"If one member suffers, all suffer together; if one member is honoured, all rejoice together." This is a law of the Christian life, and in this sense we can say that there is also an ecumenism of suffering: just as the blood of the martyrs was a seed of strength and fertility for the Church, so too the sharing of daily sufferings can become an effective instrument of unity.[100]

While the solidarity that results from such situations is positive, still we can see there is still a pressing need for the international community to ensure the right of religious freedom in national legislation and make sure that it is observed in practice. Politicians must take these issues seriously and understand the religious dimension of violence against minority groups. When a suicide bombing at a Coptic Orthodox Church in northern Egypt, in which twenty-three people were killed, prompted EU politicians to produce a draft statement on the protection of religious minorities, Baroness Ashton, EU High Representative for Foreign Affairs, refused to let any specific religious group be named.[101] This is indicative of how religious freedom has been seen as a deeply unfashionable cause for politicians to involve themselves with - even though it is enshrined in the Universal Declaration of Human Rights - and even when its violation leads to the blood of minority faiths being spilt.

Until nations take Article 18 seriously, such attacks will not be taken seriously either, or they will be played down. We have not put behind us the horrors that led to the Universal Declaration being written, and we may yet see worse horrors emerging as the lives of members of religious minorities are seen as less valuable and less human.

Conclusion

Two general points can be drawn from *Dignitatis Humanae* which, broadly speaking, underlie all Catholic thinking on the subject of religious freedom. First, secular states should grant religious freedom to everyone who lives in them. By religious freedom the Church means that no one should be coerced in religious matters, either to hold - or indeed not to hold - a set of beliefs or propositions. It is absolutely imperative that no one should be coerced or forced to act in a manner contrary to his or her beliefs.[102] Legislation designed to curb religious expressions or influence people against certain forms of religious practice are wrong, unless the practices clearly pose a threat to society. Individuals must be free to follow their informed consciences in matters relating to belief. This includes subtle forms of coercion which would make it harder for individuals to practise or manifest their religion. This freedom from coercion is based on the principles of natural law and is therefore defensible by reason alone without any recourse to divine revelation. Broadly speaking, this idea is strongly paralleled in the UN Declaration on Human Rights and represents common ground between the Church and secular notions of religious freedom.

Fr John Courtney Murray elucidated the Church's teaching on coercion:

> But such coercion can be of two kinds: a Man can be forced to act against his own beliefs, or he can somehow be forcibly denied the practice of his own beliefs or the free exercise of those beliefs. The basis or foundation of religious freedom is simply the dignity of the human person: not the subjective state of the individual conscience, mind you, but the objective truth of the human person's dignity. In particular, this objective truth of the dignity of the human person demands that, especially in religious matters, a Man should act upon his own judgement with responsible freedom, not under coercion but out of a sense of his own personal conviction with regard to his own duty. This is the basic foundation of the doctrine set forth in this Declaration.[103]

Sadly, the following words of *Dignitatis Humanae*, written around fifty years ago, are still true today: "forms of government still exist under which, even though freedom of religious worship receives constitutional recognition, the powers of government are engaged in the effort to deter citizens from the profession of religion and to make life very difficult and dangerous for religious communities."[104] And as shown above in case after case, people are forced to act against their conscience, prevented from worshipping freely, even to the extent of having places of worship burnt down.

Ultimately religious freedom as we have described it here it is a negative right - the right not to be coerced.[105] But the Catholic Church also sees religion as playing a positive role in society. *Dignitatis Humanae* states: "in order that relationships of peace and harmony be established and maintained…it is necessary that religious freedom be everywhere provided with an effective constitutional guarantee and that respect be shown for the high duty and right of man freely to lead his religious life in society."[106] It is important that civil authorities not only respect the rights of religious groups, but that they allow space for religious groups to nurture their members - and permit religions and their members to contribute to society, whether through their charitable works, their socially orientated institutions, or by the insights and wisdom they may have to offer society at large. Again, the idea of groups being free to "manifest" religion in the Declaration of Human Rights can be seen as encompassing these sorts of areas.

As Benedict XVI said, religious liberty "should be understood, then, not merely as immunity from coercion, but even more fundamentally as an ability to order one's own choices in accordance with truth".[107] And for the Church freedom is ultimately there to lead us all to *the* truth, Jesus Christ.

This then brings us to the second point, which is that the Catholic Church treasures the divine mandate that she has received from Our Lord and Saviour Jesus Christ. On the basis of divine revelation, she claims for herself the liberty to announce the Good News that God has become man in Jesus Christ and that he has risen from the dead, holding out the promise of new life for all who are incorporated into his Mystical Body. Again, as Fr Murray said:

> Truth for the Catholic is not a vague abstraction, but is concretely the revelation of Jesus Christ. Indeed the Declaration further asserts the Catholic conviction that "the one true religion subsists in the Catholic and apostolic Church, to which the Lord Jesus entrusted the task of spreading this religion among all men"…neither the spirit of ecumenism nor the principle of religious freedom requires that we cover over what we honestly believe the Church to be.[108]

Glossary of Terms

Apostolic Administrator
A priest who oversees a diocese or other pastoral area. Usually a bishop, but can be another clergyman. Apostolic Administrators may be appointed to oversee a diocese if the bishop retires or otherwise steps down, e.g. because of ill health.

Coercion
Forcing an individual or group to act against their wishes, whether through threats, physical force or any other means.

Coptic Orthodox Church
An Oriental Orthodox Church - i.e. part of that family of Churches which separated after the Council of Chalcedon in 451 AD - it traces itself back to the missionary work of St Mark in the first century. There are around eighteen million Coptic Orthodox Christians in the world, with more than ten million living in Egypt.

Gulag
The name for the forced labour camps operated by Communist authorities in the USSR from the 1930s to 1950s. Originally it referred to the agency that ran the camps. Among those interred were dissidents and political prisoners who opposed the Communist Party.

Jihadist
"Jihad" means a struggle whether a military one or an internal spiritual one. Jihadist is usually used to refer to an individual who tries to advance Islamic principles through militaristic means.

Libertas Ecclesiae
Given the divine mandate Jesus entrusted to the Church, earthly powers should grant it freedom within human society to carry out its mission. St Thomas Becket's clash with King Henry II, which led to his martyrdom in 1118, was over the rights of the Church to fulfil its sacred mandate without state intervention.

Islamist
One who believes that the Islamic faith should determine the political and social nature of society. Many Islamists would be looking for the full implementation of *Shariah* law, although various schools will interpret aspects of *Shariah* differently.

Maturidi School of Theology
One of the two main schools of systematic theology in Sunni Islam. It is based upon the writings of the scholar Abu Mansur Al Maturidi. It stresses the ability of human reason to discern the existence of God and basic moral laws without divine revelation.

Mirari Vos

An encyclical issued by Pope Gregory XVI. Promulgated on the Feast of the Assumption (15th August) 1832, it rebutted ideas of liberalism and religious indifferentism (the doctrine that salvation could be achieved regardless of religious profession) which were then current in France.

Natural Law

An objective, universal moral and ethical code. St Thomas Aquinas described natural law as "nothing else than the rational creature's participation in the eternal law" as prescribed by God, our creator (*Summa Theologica* I-II.94).

Pacem in Terris

An encyclical issued by Pope St John XXIII. Promulgated on Maundy Thursday (11th April) 1963, it looked at efforts to establish universal peace "in truth, justice, charity and liberty". It was the first papal encyclical addressed to all "men of goodwill" and not just to Catholics.

Rohingya

A predominantly Muslim ethnic minority in Rakhine state, Burma (Mynamar), numbering around one million. They have experienced abuse and discrimination, e.g. the 1982 Burmese Citizenship Act denied them citizenship. In 2012, about 140,000 Rohingya ended up in camps after their homes were destroyed during attacks by Buddhists.

Shi'a Muslims

Along with Sunni Islam, one of the two main groups in the Islamic religion. Main differences centre around the main religious authority following the death of the Prophet Mohammed - Shi'as believe his son-in-law and cousin Ali was the rightful successor - and their reverence for the shrines of their key religious figures.

Syriac-Catholic Church

One of the Eastern Churches in full communion with the Pope. It follows an ancient Syriac liturgy and is present across the Middle East, as well as in the Americas, Australasia, and some countries in western Europe.

Uighur Muslims

Uighurs are the indigenous ethnic minority in China's western Xinjiang region. Religiously, Uighurs are traditionally Muslim. Xinjiang is officially an autonomous region, like Tibet, but there are tensions between the native Uighurs and the Han Chinese whom the central government in Beijing has settled in the region.

Ukrainian Greek-Catholic Church

One of the largest of the Eastern Churches in full communion with the Pope, with more than four-and-a-half million faithful. It follows the Byzantine liturgy, employed by most Eastern Orthodox Churches, and is present in the Americas, Australasia, France and Great Britain, as well as Eastern Europe.

Universal Declaration of Human Rights

A charter adopted by the General Assembly of the United Nations on 10th December 1948, intended to guarantee certain rights to every individual everywhere. The Declaration has inspired a number of legally binding international human-rights treaties.

Endnotes

[1] My thanks to Professor Thomas Pink of King's College London, John Pontifex and Peter Sefton-Williams of Aid to the Church in Need, and staff at CTS for their comments on earlier drafts of this work.

[2] John Pontifex and John Newton, *Persecuted and Forgotten? A Report on Christians oppressed for their Faith. 2011-2013* (London, Aid to the Church in Need (UK), 2013), p. 123 *<www.acnuk.org/data/files/ resources/987/ACN_Persecuted_and_Forgotten_report_2013.pdf>* accessed 11/04/15.

[3] BBC News (online), 28/03/14, *<www.bbc.co.uk/news/world-asia-2678 1731>* accessed 11/04/15.

[4] "Pakistani Christian Still Hopeful for Release Despite Death Sentence", *Zenit*, 04/11/14.

[5] "GTA pastor confirmed held in North Korea", *Toronto Star*, 05/13/15.

[6] David Hawk, *The Hidden Gulag,* Second Edition (Washington, DC, Committee for Human Rights in North Korea, 2012), p. 4.

[7] "80 Executed Publicly in North Korea, Several For Possessing Bibles", Zenit, 12/11/13.

[8] Attilio Tamburrini (ed.), *Religious Freedom in the World - Report 2012* (Konigstein, ACN (International), 2012), p. 463; BBC News (online) 15/01/13.

[9] Pope Francis, Address for the official visit of Giorgio Napolitano, president of the Republic of Italy (08/06/13).

[10] Cf. *Catechism of the Catholic Church*, 1700; *Compendium of the Social Doctrine of the Church* (Vatican City, Libreria Editrice Vaticana, 2004), pp. 62-65. See also the Universal Declaration of Human Dignity *<http:// www.dignitatishumanae.com/index.php/declaration/>* accessed 11/04/15.

64

[11] Genesis 1:26-27, Revised Standard Version (Catholic Edition). In all quotes where "man" refers to the whole human race, or can apply equally to a man or a woman, I have silently introduced a capital "M" in to the text to highlight this.

[12] Psalm 8 quoted by Pope John XXIII, *Pacem in Terris*, 3.

[13] Cf. *Catechism of the Catholic Church*, 306.

[14] Congregation for the Doctrine of the Faith, *Liberté Religieuse: Réponse aux dubia présenté s par SE Mgr Lefebvre* (afterwards "*Dubia*"), p. 8; *Catechism of the Catholic Church*, 356-57.

[15] *Dubia*, p. 7.

[16] Cf. *Familiaris Consortio*, 22; *Gaudium et Spes*, 24.

[17] *Compendium of the Social Doctrine of the Church*, pp. 84-85.

[18] Cf. *Catechism of the Catholic Church*, 1778. Moreover, God has stamped a moral order on our inmost, which is revealed to us by our conscience - "a law inscribed by God" (*Gaudium et Spes*, 16).

[19] *Catechism of the Catholic Church*, 1798.

[20] *Dignitatis Humanae*, 3.

[21] Tamburrini, *Religious Freedom in the World - Report 2012*, p. 465; *Scottish Catholic Observer*, 24/04/13.

[22] Cf. *Dignitatis Humanae*, 3.

[23] Pope John XXIII, *Pacem in Terris*, 14 citing Lactantius, *Divinae Institutiones*, IV:28.2 and Pope Leo XIII, *Libertas Praestantissimum*, 30.

[24] The word "religion" probably comes from the Latin *religare*, which means to tie or to bind.

[25] *Dignitatis Humanae*, 3.

[26] *Dignitatis Humanae*, 1. It is also important to note the following sentence: "Therefore it leaves untouched traditional Catholic doctrine on the moral duty of men and societies toward the true religion and toward the one Church of Christ." Properly understood and rightly interpreted, *Dignitatis Humanae* is in full continuity with the magisterium of the Church and must be read that way. See the section, "Council teaching, a break with tradition?".

[27] *Dignitatis Humanae*, 2, italics mine.

[28] Ibid., 2.

[29] BBC News (online), 20/01/12; Al Jazeera, 15/06/12.

[30] Pope John XXIII, *Pacem in Terris*, 34, 48.

[31] "Chinese authorities block pilgrimage to Marian Shrine in Donglu", Asia News, 27/05/13.

[32] *Dignitatis Humanae*, 3.

[33] *Dignitatis Humanae*, 4 as is all material in the points listed below, except where noted.

[34] Pontifex and Newton, *Persecuted and Forgotten? 2011-2013*, p. 38.

[35] Asia News, 21/05/14, 23/12/14; China Aid, 12/12/14; Tom Phillips, "China destroys statues as 'anti-Christian' campaign widens", *Daily Telegraph*, 01/05/14.

[36] Rachel Ritchie, "Zhejiang court sentences 8 Christians from Sanjiang Church", *China Aid*, 26/03/15 <http://www.chinaaid.org/2015/03/eight-zhejiang-christians-from-sanjiang.html> accessed 14/04/15.

[37] Here I have departed from the English translation of *Dignitatis Humanae* found on the Holy See's website. The Latin reads: "Communitates religiosae ius etiam habent, ne impediantur in sua fide ore et scripto publice docenda atque testanda." The use of "manifest" is brought out in the French translation: "Les communautés religieuses ont aussi le droit de ne pas être empêchées d'enseigner et de **manifester** leur foi publiquement, de vive voix et par écrit." I have preferred this because of the use of the term "manifest" in the Universal Declaration of Human Rights.

[38] *Dignitatis Humanae*, 4.

[39] Nguyen Hung, "Land seized from nuns to build a 4-star hotel", Asia News, 20/05/2008.

[40] Ideas of the universality of natural law were reaffirmed by Pope St John Paul II, "Inasmuch as [the natural law] is inscribed in the rational nature of the person, it makes itself felt to all beings endowed with reason and living in history. In order to perfect himself in his specific order, the person must do good and avoid evil, be concerned for the transmission and preservation of life, refine and develop the riches of the material world, cultivate social life, seek truth, practise good and contemplate beauty." *Veritatis Splendor*, 51.

[41] United States Commission on International Religious Freedom, Annual Report 2013, p 30.

[42] "'Underage' Tibetan Monks Face New Clampdown on Religious Life", Radio Free Asia, 24/02/15, <www.rfa.org/english/news/tibet/underage-02242015155409.html> accessed 11/04/15.

[43] Martin Patience, "China Xinjiang: Muslim students 'made to eat' at Ramadan", BBC News (online) China Blog, 11/07/14; Adam Withnall, "China bans Ramadan", *Independent*, 03/07/14.

[44] *Dignitatis Humanae*, 14.

66

[45] Pope John Paul II, *Redemptor Hominis*, 17.

[46] Pope Benedict XVI, Message for World Peace Day (01/01/11), 1.

[47] Pontifex and Newton, *Persecuted and Forgotten? 2011 Edition*, p. 71.

[48] "Iraq" in *Religious Freedom in the World - Report 2010* edited by Attilio Tamburrini (Konigstein, ACN (International), 2010, issued as CD ROM.

[49] Rupert Shortt, "Christians persecuted throughout the world", *Daily Telegraph*, 29/10/12 and other sources.

[50] Pontifex and Newton, *Persecuted and Forgotten? 2011-2013*, pp. 28 ff; pp. 136 ff.

[51] Ibid., p. 29.

[52] United States Conference of Catholic Bishops Ad Hoc Committee on Religious Liberty, *Our First, Most Cherished Liberty: A Statement on Religious Liberty*, 12/04/12.

[53] Cf. Article 18 of the UN International Covenant on Civil and Political Rights.

[54] Archbishop Silvano M. Tomasi (permanent observer of the Holy See to the United Nations), Speech given during the course of the nineteenth ordinary session of the Human Rights Council (01/03/12).

[55] *Dignitatis Humanae*, 7.

[56] Pope Benedict XVI, Message for 2011 World Peace Day (01/01/11), 7. (Italics removed).

[57] *Dignitatis Humanae*, 7.

[58] See *Catechism of the Catholic Church*, 2108.

[59] *Dignitatis Humanae*, 1.

[60] Ibid., 8.

[61] Ibid., 6.

[62] Ibid., 3.

[63] Ibid., 5.

[64] Genesis 18:19.

[65] This idea is not my own and was suggested in Jonathan Sacks, "Credo", *The Times*, 27/07/13, p. 75.

[66] United Nations, Universal Declaration of Human Rights, Article 26:3.

[67] The English word education comes from the Latin *educere*, which means "to draw forth".

[68] *Compendium*, 239, citing *Gravissimum Educationis*, 3; John Paul II, Apostolic Exhortation *Familiaris Consortio*, 36.

[69] Holy See, *Charter of the Rights of the Family*, 5b.

[70] *Dignitatis Humanae*, 5.

[71] Cf. Congregation for the Doctrine of the Faith, *Libertatis Conscientia*, 94.

[72] John Pontifex and John Newton, *Persecuted and Forgotten? A report on Christians oppressed for their Faith. 2011 Edition* (London, Aid to the Church in Need (UK), 2011), p. 128.

[73] John Newton and Martin Kugler, "Western Europe" in *Religious Freedom in the World - Report 2014* edited by John Pontifex (Konigstein, Germany, Aid to the Church in Need (International)) <*religion-freedom-report.org.uk/wp-content/uploads/country-reports/regional-analysis/western_europe.pdf*> accessed 11/04/15.

[74] Pope Benedict XVI, Message for World Peace Day (01/01/11), 4.

[75] Pope John Paul II, *Redemptor Hominis*, 17.

[76] *Dignitatis Humanae*, 13.

[77] *Dubia*, p. 12.

[78] Ibid., p. 10.

[79] Pope Leo XIII, *Immortale Dei*, 36.

[80] Ibid., 4. Cf. *Ad Gentes*, 13.

[81] Pope Paul VI, *Evangelii Nuntiandi*, 80.

[82] Cf. ibid., 14.

[83] Edward Gaffey, "Religious Liberty and Development of Doctrine: An Interview with John C. Murray", *Catholic World*, 204 (February 1967), pp. 277-83. <*http://woodstock.georgetown.edu/library/murray/1967i.htm*> [italics mine]. While we must admit Fr Murray's expertise in this field and his influence following the Council (for example, he wrote the introduction and commentary in the most popular English translation of Vatican II's documents), it should be remembered that some of Fr Murray's views were rejected by Council Fathers during Vatican II's debate on religious liberty. Indeed, in 1954 he had been silenced for his views on the subject, when they were thought to contradict Church teaching. However, it should equally be stressed that he faithfully accepted the silencing, remaining loyal to the Church. It would be utterly wrong to depict Fr Murray as some sort of dissident theologian, although it should be remembered that his personal theological opinions were found wanting in some points by the Church.

[84] Pope John XXIII, *Pacem in Terris*, 42.

[85] *Dubia*, p. 23.

[86] Pope Benedict XVI, *Caritas in Veritate*, 55.

68

[87] *Dignitatis Humanae*, 1.

[88] Ibid., 15.

[89] Pope John XXIII, *Pacem in Terris*, 144.

[90] Pope Benedict XVI, Address to members of the General Assembly of the UN (18/04/08).

[91] Ibid.

[92] Pew Research Centre's Forum on Religion and Public Life, *Rising Restrictions on Religion* (Washington, Pew Research Centre, 2011), pp. 7, 98.

[93] Archbishop Silvano M. Tomasi, Speech given during the course of the nineteenth ordinary session of the Human Rights Council (01/03/12).

[94] Pope John Paul II, *Redemptor Hominis*, 17.

[95] Ibid., 17.

[96] John Newton, "Tributes paid as Cardinal who survived the gulags dies", ACN News, 22/07/11.

[97] Neville Kirk-Smith, *You are the hands of Christ in Eastern Europe* (Aid to the Church in Need report), edited by John Newton (Sutton, ACN (UK), 2011), p. 4.

[98] Michele Clark and Nadia Ghaly, *The Disappearance, Forced Conversions, and Forced Marriages of Coptic Christian Women in Egypt* (Christian Solidarity International & Coptic Foundation for Human Rights, 2009) <*www.coptsunited.com/Uploads/40/Coptic_Report_Master.pdf*> accessed 11/04/15.

[99] *The Christian Post*, 04/09/13.

[100] Pope Francis, Address to Pope Tawadros II, Head of the Coptic Orthodox Church of Egypt, 10/05/13. Quotation from 1 Corinthians, 12:26.

[101] "Italy blocks EU religious persecution text ignoring Christians", *Reuters*, 31/01/11.

[102] *Dignitatis Humanae*, 2.

[103] Gaffey, "Religious Liberty and Development of Doctrine", *Catholic World*, 204.

[104] *Dignitatis Humanae*, 15.

[105] *Dubia*, p. 10.

[106] *Dignitatis Humanae*, 15.

[107] Pope Benedict XVI, Message for the 2011 World Day of Peace.

[108] Gaffey, "Religious Liberty and Development of Doctrine", *Catholic World*, 204.

A Guide to Religious Freedom and the Law

Neil Addison

This booklet considers areas of the law relating to Religious Freedom and Discrimination, which are of specific interest to Catholic institutions and individual Catholics; in particular the exemptions in Discrimination law which apply to religious organisations in England, Wales and Scotland. The author offers a helpful introductory tour of the key issues and areas to be aware of, primarily for a Catholic audience though it may well be of assistance to members of other religions and Churches since many of the legal questions are common across religious boundaries.

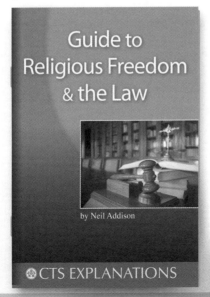

Guide to
Religious Freedom
& the Law

by Neil Addison

⦿ CTS EXPLANATIONS

EX49   ISBN 978 1 86082 908 6

Oscar Romero

Fr Ashley Beck

Throughout history Christians have suffered martyrdom
and torture as a result of 'hatred of the faith' (odium fidei).
Archbishop Oscar Romero, gunned down while saying
Mass, was declared to be such a martyr by Pope Francis,
thus opening the way for his beatification. Romero paid
the ultimate price for his faithfulness to Christ and his
Church, rather than is often misrepresented, for his
political activism. Romero's impressive body of teaching,
personal holiness and sufferings illustrate what an
impressive witness to the faith he truly was.

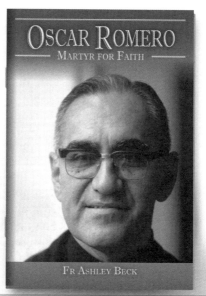

B700   ISBN 971 78469 059 5

Cardinal Nguyen Van Thuan

Helena Scott / Ethel Tolanski

In 1975 as the Communists finally overtook South Vietnam, Archbishop Thuan was picked up in Saigon and began 13 years of imprisonment, including several years in solitary confinement. Highly intelligent, able and gifted, and above all a man of deep faith, Thuan's spiritual journey - along with his life before and after - is chronicled here. Thuan's story has become a remarkable testimony to Christian love, fortitude and forgiveness, where the light of hope never dims. In 2001, John Paul II made him a Cardinal. He died the following year.

CARDINAL NGUYEN VAN THUAN

♫ CTS BIOGRAPHIES ♫

BY ETHEL TOLANSKY & HELENA SCOTT

B721   ISBN 978 1 86082 583 5

change the basic truth that God made us to resemble him. As St Thomas Aquinas wrote, even if you are sin you are still made in the image of God. So the *Catechism of the Catholic Church* teaches, "Since every person created by God has the basic dignity of being created in the image of God and is sacred, this dignity cannot be lost."[14] Through the fall humanity may have lost its supernatural dignity, but not its natural dignity.[15] This transcendent dignity is the basis of all rights and responsibilities.[16] Thus the ultimate source of human rights is not the fickle will of human beings, nor the state, nor public powers, but God.[17] Following from this fundamental dignity of the human individual, there are two basic freedoms which underpin the right to religious liberty within a modern society: freedom from coercion by the state and freedom of conscience.

Freedom of Conscience

Freedom not to be forced to act against our conscience is key to the Church's teaching on the role of religious liberty in a civil society. But what is meant by conscience? Conscience is a judgement of our reason whereby we recognise the moral quality of our actions, whether those we are going to do, those we are in the act of doing, or those we have already done.[18] "A well-formed conscience is upright and truthful. It formulates its judgements according to reason, in conformity with the true good willed by the wisdom of the Creator."[19] In all we do and say we are obliged to follow what we know to be just and right. It is therefore fundamentally wrong to force anyone to act in ways which violate what they believe. So the Church teaches that no one should be coerced to acts in a manner contrary to their conscience.[20] Many of the laws and structures of society in western countries have, over the course of the last hundred years, recognised that some practices within society are seen as morally objectionable by members of those societies - in many of these cases, the Church would argue certain practices are objectively morally wrong, but that's another argument, which we don't have room to discuss here - and has sought to provide protection for people's consciences. But it isn't always straightforward in practice.

Freedom of conscience refused

In Scotland, devout Catholic midwives Mary Doogan, aged fifty-seven, and Concepta Wood, aged fifty-one, went to law in 2012 to avoid having to oversee staff carrying out abortions at Southern General Hospital, Glasgow. Under UK law they can register their conscientious objections to take part in abortion procedures - and had done so - but found themselves overseeing staff involved with medical terminations after staffing structures were re-arranged. They ended up in a position they objected to on moral grounds and, after the NHS argued their rights of conscience only extended to direct participation in abortions, they went to law to argue their case. They lost their initial court case but won on appeal.

The appeal judges (Lady Dorrian, sitting with Lord Mackay of Drumadoon and Lord McEwan) ruled that,

> the right of conscientious objection extends not only to the actual medical or surgical termination but to the whole process of treatment given for that purpose. The right is given because it is recognised that the process of abortion is felt by many people to be morally repugnant. The right of conscientious objection is given out of respect for those convictions and not for any other reason. It is in keeping with the reason for the exemption that the wide interpretation which we favour should be given to it.

However, the NHS went to the UK Supreme Court to stop conscientious objections applying in such cases, and in December 2014 the court ruled that Mary Doogan and Concepta Wood must supervise nurses involved in carrying out abortions, even if they morally object to these procedures.

Mario Conti, the then Archbishop of Glasgow, reflected:

It is fundamental to the functioning of society that all citizens act in accordance with an informed conscience. Any law or judgement which fails to recognise this contradicts that most basic freedom and duty which we all have as human beings, namely to follow our conscience and act accordingly.[21]

Freedom to seek the Truth

We must be free to follow our conscience as our conscience will help to lead us towards God.[22] And when it comes to religion, our acceptance of God must be true, sincere and free. This teaching of *Dignitatis Humanae* on conscience flows from well-established magisterial teaching on the subject, which at the time of the Second Vatican Council had most recently been articulated in Pope St John XXIII's encyclical *Pacem in Terris*: [23]

Also among Man's rights is that of being able to worship God in accordance with the right dictates of his own conscience, and to profess his religion both in private and in public. According to the clear teaching of [the third-century Christian writer] Lactantius, "this is the very condition of our birth, that we render to the God who made us that just homage which is his due; that we acknowledge him alone as God, and follow him. It is from this ligature of piety, which binds us and joins us to God, that religion derives its name."[24]

Hence, too, Pope Leo XIII declared that "true freedom, freedom worthy of the sons of God, is that freedom which most truly safeguards the dignity of the human person. It is stronger than any violence or injustice. Such is the freedom which has always been desired by the Church, and which she holds most dear. It is the sort of freedom which the Apostles resolutely claimed for themselves. The apologists defended it in their writings; thousands of martyrs consecrated it with their blood."

This theme is taken up and expounded in *Dignitatis Humanae*:

In all his activity a Man is bound to follow his conscience in order that he may come to God, the end and purpose of life. It follows that he is not to be forced to act in a manner contrary to his conscience. Nor, on the other hand, is he to be restrained from acting in accordance

---

[24] The word "religion" probably comes from the Latin *religare*, which means to tie or to bind.

with his conscience, especially in matters religious. The reason is that the exercise of religion, of its very nature, consists before all else in those internal, voluntary and free acts whereby Man sets the course of his life directly toward God. No merely human power can either command or prohibit acts of this kind.[25]

Freedom from Coercion

Building on the Church's belief in the dignity of the human being, the central plank of the Church's teaching on religious liberty can be found in *Dignitatis Humanae*, where it states that: "Religious freedom...which men demand as necessary to fulfil their duty to worship God, has to do with immunity from coercion in civil society."[26] It goes on to add:

> [A]ll men should be at once impelled by nature and also bound by a moral obligation to seek the truth, especially religious truth. They are also bound to adhere to the truth, once it is known, and to order their whole lives in accord with the demands of truth. *However, men cannot discharge these obligations* in a manner in keeping with their own nature *unless they enjoy immunity from external coercion* as well as psychological freedom.[27]

Again the Church's teaching - whilst it has wider implications for the way that all religions and all individuals

---

[26] It is also important to note the following sentence: "Therefore it leaves untouched traditional Catholic doctrine on the moral duty of men and societies toward the true religion and toward the one Church of Christ." Properly understood and rightly interpreted, *Dignitatis Humanae* is in full continuity with the magisterium of the Church and must be read that way. See the section, "Council teaching, a break with tradition?".

should receive respect and tolerance - views the issue through the prism of the Faith, and sees all of these aspects as related to individuals' fundamental relationship to the God who created them. As described above, the Catholic view of humanity is that we were made for God and all of these freedoms exist that his creatures may find him and know him.

Dignitatis Humanae goes on to define exactly what was meant by religious freedom, stating that it meant that everyone is,

> to be immune from coercion on the part of individuals or of social groups and of any human power, in such wise that no one is to be forced to act in a manner contrary to his own beliefs, whether privately or publicly, whether alone or in association with others, within due limits.[28]

Again we see echoes of the importance the Church places on conscience which we explored above. Essentially, in matters of belief, people should not be coerced by the state, by other civil institutions, nor by groups or individuals acting of their own volition. While the individual examples of violations of religious freedom given so far have concentrated on cases where Christians have experienced problems it should be obvious that Church teaching applies to all forms of belief, and so the Church would equally deplore cases such as that of Indonesian atheist Alexander An, who was sentenced to two and a half years in jail and fined more than $10,000 for professing his disbelief in God on the internet.[29] A secular state has no right to attempt to coerce someone to believe - or not believe - by using the force of law.

Writing just two years before *Dignitatis Humanae*, Pope St John XXIII said:

> Man's personal dignity requires besides that he enjoy freedom and be able to make up his own mind when he acts...Each man should act on his own initiative, conviction, and sense of responsibility, not under the constant pressure of external coercion or enticement. There is nothing human about a society that is welded together by force. Far from encouraging, as it should, the attainment of Man's progress and perfection, it is merely an obstacle to his freedom.

He added, "a regime which governs solely or mainly by means of threats and intimidation or promises of reward... would certainly be offensive to the dignity of free and rational human beings."[30] The case of the imprisoned atheist is repugnant to anyone who thinks through the issues involved, even if they do not agree with his personal beliefs.

Rights of religious groups

Since 1996, authorities in China's Hebei Province have stopped Catholic pilgrims going to the church in Donglu for an annual feast celebrating an apparition of Our

20

Lady there in 1900. According to reports, police set up
checkpoints on the roads into the town and manned these
around the clock with armed guards.[31] For the Catholic
Church, the right to gather together for worship - whether
at a sacred site for big annual feasts, or week by week in
local communities - is a basic part of religious freedom.
Humans are social creatures; we come together in groups
to pursue common goals, and our "social nature" means
we also want to profess our religion as part of a group.[32]

So it follows that the rights of communities are also very
important. If we restrict religious freedom to individuals
we deny this important social dimension of religion. This
is why *Dignitatis Humanae* goes on to say that religious
communities "rightfully claim" freedom from state and
civil coercion in order that they may govern their activities
according to their own convictions and principles,
worship God, help their members in their religious lives,
particularly by religious instruction; and meet together to
order their lives in accordance with their beliefs.[33]

Such communities have the right:
1. Not to be hindered, either by legal measures or by
administrative action by the government:

   • in the selection, training, appointment, and transferral
   of their own ministers

   • in communicating with religious authorities and
   communities abroad

• in erecting buildings for religious purposes

• in acquiring and using suitable properties

• in acquiring and using suitable funds.

To use China as an example again, the state has denied many of the basic freedoms listed above. Catholic churches are not free to communicate with the Vatican, and the state intervenes in many aspects of Church life. Authorities will often impose their own candidates as bishops over the will of both the local Church and the Vatican - and numerous priests were detained by police or ejected from their parishes in July 2012 after they objected to the episcopal ordination of Fr Joseph Yue Fusheng as Bishop of Harbin. Fr Fusheng had been forced on the Catholic diocese by the state without Vatican approval. [34]

Using buildings for religious purposes can also be a contentious issue in China. Not only have religious organisations been stopped from buying properties or land to build on, but existing places of worship have been seized by the state. In 2014, at least twelve churches were pulled down in Zhejiang Province and more than 420 churches had their crosses removed. [35] In some cases congregations organised demonstrations as officials tried to destroy buildings or remove crosses. In March 2015, eight Christians who had protested over plans to demolish their church were given prison sentences for "gathering a crowd to disturb public order". Despite their objections their church was razed to the ground and replaced by a fruit orchard.[36]

2. Not to be prevented from publicly speaking and writing in order to manifest and teach about their own faith.[37]

This is important because it stresses that this is not about communities being free to worship behind closed doors, but rather that faith communities should be allowed to participate fully in a democratic society. Religious communities have the right not to be hindered from publicly teaching and speaking about their faith - for example, they should be able to arrange public lectures about their beliefs and to print and propagate literature about what they believe.

Dignitatis Humanae also stresses that in spreading their beliefs faith communities should not use coercion or "dishonourable persuasion" in order to gain adherents as an individual must freely respond to the call of God. The Church teaches that "in spreading religious faith and in introducing religious practices everyone ought at all times to refrain from any manner of action which might seem to carry a hint of coercion or of a kind of persuasion that would be dishonourable or unworthy, especially when dealing with poor or uneducated people. Such a manner of action would have to be considered an abuse of one's right and a violation of the right of others."[38] Although "dishonourable persuasion" is not defined, presumably it suggests practices such as only giving the hungry food if they first sit through a talk about the group's beliefs.

3. Not be prohibited from freely undertaking to show the special value of their doctrine in what concerns the organisation of society and the inspiration of the whole of human activity.

For example, the Church has salient views on moral and social issues and should be free to make its position known.

4. Not be prevented from freely holding meetings.

5. Not be stopped from establishing educational, cultural, charitable and social organisations "under the impulse of their own religious sense".

This would refer to religious groups setting up schools, hospitals, overseas relief and development charities, and other organisations which reflect their own ethos and embody their own particular values. This right would prohibit actions such as the demolishing a convent and orphanage in Vinh Long, southern Vietnam in 2008 - which had been previously seized by local authorities - so that a four-star hotel could be built.[39]

Natural Law

The Catholic Church sees the above rights as being defensible on the basis of natural law - and it is worth briefly explaining what natural law is. Natural law is the concept that certain rights or values are universal, being discernible by human reason as it observes the natural order of the universe. Human reason can ascertain certain principles of justice and injustice which are universal, apply to the entire human race, and are binding on everyone.[40] Ideas of natural law are not unique to the Catholic Church. They first appear in the classical philosophers and while employed by various Church Fathers, natural law has been widely used both in non-Christian religious and in secular thought. In Islam's Maturidi School of theology, it was posited that the human mind could discern the existence of God - and indeed most objective standards of good and evil - by reason alone. Secular thought has long valued the idea of natural law and until the mid-twentieth century the concept of natural law still underlay most legal systems, and many state constitutions were ostensibly based on it.

---

[40] Ideas of the universality of natural law were reaffirmed by Pope St John Paul II, "Inasmuch as [the natural law] is inscribed in the rational nature of the person, it makes itself felt to all beings endowed with reason and living in history. In order to perfect himself in his specific order, the person must do good and avoid evil, be concerned for the transmission and preservation of life, refine and develop the riches of the material world, cultivate social life, seek truth, practise good and contemplate beauty." *Veritatis Splendor*, 51.

So the Church is saying that by human reason, without recourse to divine revelation, we can deduce the importance of the right to freedom from state coercion in religious matters. If you reason it through, you can see that the only way to prevent religious groups from carrying out these activities would be to force them in some way. For example, if a society is determined to stop people from freely meeting to worship it will ultimately have to send in police or even the military to stop them from doing so. The Church argues that on rational grounds such draconian measures by the state are unjust, except where the group's activities pose a tangible danger to individuals or groups.

Coercion Today

But in many countries coercion is used to restrict religion in line with the state's ideology. As indicated above, authorities in many of China's provinces continue to interfere forcibly in religious matters. Severe restrictions are placed on religious groups and individuals whose practices are deemed to exceed the vague legal definition of "normal religious activities". These restrictions include harassment, detention, imprisonment, and other abuses. China's government has imprisoned religious leaders and ministers, attempted to control the selection of clergy, and banned religious gatherings. Religious freedom restrictions for Tibetan Buddhists and Uighur Muslims remain particularly acute.[41] In February 2015 young Buddhist monks under the age of nineteen, who had returned home for the Tibetan New Year, were instructed by authorities in Qinghai Province to stop their religious training and enrol in local state schools, rather than continuing their education in the monasteries where they had been studying.[42] Similarly Muslim students and government workers in Xinjiang Province were stopped from observing the Ramadan Fast by officials in 2014, and in some areas were barred from attending Mosque services.[43] The use of extreme measures to control religion is condemned by the Catholic Church: